Transitions & Selves

Pratishtha Nahata

BookLeaf Publishing

Presentation by *BookLeaf Publishing*

Web: www.bookleafpub.com

E-mail: info@bookleafpub.com

ISBN: 9789395784559

First edition 2022

DEDICATION

To Cherry, for being my first & favourite reader

Missing home

It's been some time
Some time away from home
I left to chase dreams
To explore, to roam

Everything I could ever want
I got it all
My branches bear fruit
They stand proud, and tall

It's been some time
And I now miss home
My roots need watering
Some love, some loam.

Looking for something: where do we go?

Am I looking for a message?
Or perhaps a key?
Some sense of direction,
Of where I'm supposed to be?

Perhaps I'm seeking adventure
In music, travel, prose;
Or through a pretend door
To sneak out of, on tip-toes

Perhaps it's somewhere obvious,
a place I've seen in dreams..
Where my head & heart are not
playing for different teams.

Under the sea

Here we go again,
chasing treasures
Deep in the oceans,
uncharted, unmeasured

A sparkle here,
a twinkle there
Moments later,
we're in Ursula's lair

She laughs, at our fear
& offers us tea
"These trinkets mean nothing,
it's you, you see"

We rise up to the surface,
lost & unsure
And it dawns on us,
what our journey was for

She was right, we find
Treasure wasn't down there
It was in being alive & in love,
In our ability to care.

To the moon, in turbulence

I feel so permeable
Like I could disappear in you
As I scroll through my phone
Because what else could I do?

I have everything material
No signs of lack
Except my peace of mind
Of which I have lost track

"I'm free!", I think some days
But also somehow bound
In illusions, in karma,
In truth refusing to be found.

I must look inside, I know
Self-awareness the only cost
What do I do, dear moon?
When my connection to myself is lost

This moment, it stretches forever
Chaotic, turbulent, dark
As the flames die out they leave
Smoke.. but no spark

Another match drops, un-lit
I can see it one of two ways -
Potential left unfulfilled
Or a fresh new start, a new day.

PMS? Maybe.

Maybe it's the time of the month
Maybe it's the time of the year
A waning moon or equinox
A time my "self" can disappear

And in that hollow space it leaves
other voices get louder and louder
With no grounded, rooted centre,
What looked like a mountain, is all powder

A form of gluttony then appears, charging
its way through sense & taste
Knowing full well it cannot
handle or digest what it consumes in haste

I find it hard to invoke kindness
when nothing escapes this critical lens
So I try to look for the gifts
Of this mode of vision & messages it sends

It's a personal winter now
A time to reflect & face the hidden
unacknowledged anger & grief
things swept under & feelings unbidden

Comfort movies, books & food
I hope that going through these motions
Will spark my "self" back to me
& be my anchor in these oceans.

Have courage & be kind

Close your eyes
Look within
Try not to judge
No virtue, no sin

Try not to brace
You'll never be ready
To face all you find
The erratic, or the steady

Don't let that deter you
From moving ahead
Perhaps you'll find comfort
In a book you once read

Perhaps you'll fall
Into an old thinking trap
Or perhaps you'll find
A hidden treasure map

Perhaps you'll find
A giant squid or two
Just don't forget to be kind
Because, after all, it is you.

Stranger in my shoes, stranger in my life

"Open me" it says
But where is the key?

A fish out of water
Far away from the sea

A journey undertaken
Memory lost & found

I sit in this corner
Making no sound

Is this my body?
Is this my crown?

Under the weight of questions
The "I" falls down

Doing THE THING: coming back to now

Sometimes I get lost
In the future yet to come
Sometimes I find my thoughts
Have my objective self undone

I know what I must do
But I don't want to do it now
I also can't stop thinking though
If I don't, then when? And how?

A war breaks out within
And I'm frozen in place
Asking myself yet again
"What might bring me solace?"

It's an old pattern, this one
Of not trusting myself to rise
Of assuming I must carry this weight
To eventually do what's wise

And even though, not long ago
I've proven to me I'm worth the trust
To do THE THING well in time
And even enjoy it, when I must

I still fall back in these loops
But, it's not all that bad
One way around it, is to ask,
"What, right now, will make me glad?"

And then to follow my heart
to its content, unhurried
Knowing that when I immerse myself
in the present moment, I'm not worried

And I slowly soften & open
Let joy infuse my being
In the process, I re-discover
A most delightful way of seeing

That THE THING that must be done
Is in fact - a choice, not a chore
It's no longer driven by force or fear
But by love, & of that I'm sure.

An ode to improvising

Give me the stage
Let me unfold
And my dear audience
I will hold

Your attention, anticipation
Palpable, pure
And I don't know how I know
But I know this for sure

It's a beautiful moment
When I see
That you are enraptured
And you're looking back at me

Every pause as meaningful
As every word said
I speak from my heart
Instead of my head

We're aware
We're alight
Not a phone or screen
In sight

Our masks put aside
We've come out to play
And where we go from here?
Well, who can say?!

It's this unknown that holds
The fear and the magic
The delightful and the strange
The beautiful and the tragic

When we follow our curiosity
And into this unknown we delve
We find the ultimate pleasure
Of surprising ourselves

Forgiving myself for excesses

I want something to consume
I want something to read
Something to put me to sleep
I don't know what I need

My heart feels heavy
I'm running away from feeling
Running from paying attention
The only path to healing

I pushed myself too much
Even though I didn't want to
I fell into old patterns
Compelling me to "do, do! DO."

I betrayed myself here
Unsure how I will go on
In this world run on capitalism
Taking real rest, just feels wrong

Forgive me, body
Forgive me, mind & soul
I'm still working out
How to balance being whole

Strangers in my mind

Strange are the thoughts that plague my mind
Stranger than them, are the feelings behind
Cold hands, they wrap, around my heart
The cage, and the bird, playing their part

They won't, you see, they won't go away
They're here now, and they're here to stay
The eyes will look, the eyes will burn
And then maybe, one day I'll learn.

When the chill reaches my blood, my bones
And in mirrors and glasses, I see my clones
The ones I knew, the ones I did not
The ones I kept, the ones I fought

I'm afraid of them, who are they?
These voices that have such a powerful sway
On what I think & on what I do
They're not gentle, they're harsh; sometimes
cruel

They're all of us, they're all of me
They all come from different branches of a tree
I take a breath, and dig deep in here
At the roots, I find, there's nothing to fear

What look like storms, are but a projection
What seem like mountains, are mild objections
The stranger's voices, they come up at last
But what I know now is that - “this too shall pass”.

Her problem, my last

She knew then
She knew at last
Why life, once beautiful
In misery, was cast

Why colours, so brilliant
Looked pallid, and pale
Why her wandering mind
Didn't set off to sail

To unbound lands
Of imagination, raw,
Why it refused to accept
All the things she saw

Why there was no race
In thoughts she penned
Why new books, people, places
Just didn't send

A shiver of delight
Down her spine
Why her eyes and vigour
Had lost their shine

The lack of creation
And consuming too much
Had dulled her senses
Sights, tastes & touch

There was only one way out
Only one way to be -
She started writing this
And she became me.

Perfection

If you knew what it was like
To see yourself through my eyes
You would find no flaws.

The missing muse

Oh inspiration
Where are you?
I've searched far & wide
In the skies so blue

Out in the garden
And on my screens
Under the table
(Whatever that means)

The pressure is on
Time's running out
And I don't know what
I'm going to write about

Perhaps if I sit here
& stop looking for you
Let my hand take the pen
And the reigns too

Maybe you will be tempted
By the flowing ink
Maybe you'll appear
like an unexpected link

Maybe you'll buzz
In my head like a bee
Or like a forgotten penny
That "Whoa!" I suddenly see

Perhaps, the pressure will pass
Perhaps, there will be more time
Perhaps, I will find an answer
In writing about your crime

Of hiding from me so
But then redeeming yourself,
By peeking through the pages
Of a dusty book on my shelf

In this age old story
You ride the well-worn spine
And then you leap off gallantly
Making your way into my first line

I have found you at last!
But I cannot rest here -
I must write and write, and write and write,
Before once again, you disappear

[Un]Masked

Now I'm here
Now I'm not
In the blink of an eye
When you think you've got
Hold of me
I'll slip through
And what you see
Might not always be true
Light is the shadow
For things that hide
Their tentacles spread
Far, and wide
Pure in their intent
Like white flakes of snow
And when you look closely
You too, will know
There's a smile on the face
But it won't be me
It will be her
Don't believe what you see
Let me tell you this
Before you ask
Behind it you will find
Just another mask.

The emergence of a suppressed feeling

What did I do
When I already knew
The consequences of saying
What was in my heart

It wasn't a new feeling
Not even recent
Just a memory
A powerful memory

One that had been locked
Stamped down and ignored
Wrestled into smallness
But would not be contained

Biding its time
While I thought it was a cloud
One passing rarely
With a gentle, frivolous ask of "what if"

But it was really a raging wave
One determined to crash over me
When I saw you
After all these years

A wave with no concern for the present,
No care for the changes
A life of its own, confessing at will
A feeling that was, at its best, just a memory

Instructions on growing

We grow up
Then we stop
Play patterns on repeat
Until we drop

Instead of flowering
We start to harden
We grow thorns
In life's garden

We yearn for love
Yet fear being close
We forget when and how
Our hearts froze

The first step is to learn
To feel our feelings
The second is to accept them,
It's the only way of healing

The last is to realise
What growing up is about
It is not supposed to be the end,
We must strive to grow out.

Travelling worlds

1: Longing

There is this feeling
Not persistent
But a hunger, a longing
For familiarity, for home

One I forget
When I've gotten comfortable
When I've coalesced
Into a cocoon of security

One that emerges
At the cusp of a new possibility
At the end of the last road
When it's least expected

--

2: Newness

I love the newness
That travel brings
The experiences, the people,
Everything in between

How beautiful
The world can be

How treacherous
How fluidly definitive

The art, the buildings
The new shapes of leaves
The underlying oneness
That grows stronger for every difference counted

--

3: Everything

Life pauses in one place
Begins in another
But time passes by
Everywhere, all at once

Beyond the scope
Of one's own experience
Flowing, diverging, merging
Twisting, turning, evolving

And somehow in this moving space
There is a feeling of such loss
Comfortably parallel to the recognition
Of room for something more to enter

--

I live in all these different worlds..

www.ingramcontent.com/pod-product-compliance
Lightning Source LLC
Chambersburg PA
CBHW051759130826
49812CB00033B/1206
9789395784559